GREAT SCIENCE WRITERS™

ISAAC ASIMOV

PHILIP WOLNY

ROSEN
PUBLISHING®

New York

Published in 2015 by The Rosen Publishing Group, Inc.
29 East 21st Street, New York, NY 10010

Copyright © 2015 by The Rosen Publishing Group, Inc.

First Edition

Library of Congress Cataloging-in-Publication Data

Wolny, Philip, author.
Isaac Asimov/Philip Wolny.—First edition.
    pages cm.—(Great science writers)
Includes bibliographical references and index.
ISBN 978-1-4777-7689-6 (library bound)
1. Asimov, Isaac, 1920-1992—Juvenile literature. 2. Authors,
American—20th century—Biography—Juvenile literature. 3.
Science writers—United States—Biography—Juvenile litera-
ture. I. Title.
PS3551.S5Z9 2015
813.54—dc23

                                                    2013049327

Manufactured in China

CONTENTS

t was September 1963 in Washington, D.C., and the twenty-first World Science Fiction Convention (titled Discon1) was in full swing at the Statler-Hilton Hotel. Isaac Asimov, renowned and critically acclaimed for his science fiction, was toastmaster. The World Science Fiction Society gave out its annual Hugo Awards for achievements in science fiction and fantasy.

The forty-three-year-old Asimov was also famous for nonfiction writing. Thus, that night in Washington, Asimov not only amused the audience with his wit but also received his very first major award—a special Hugo for his collected science writing in the magazine *Fantasy & Science Fiction*. In 1958, he was asked to write a monthly column of up to four thousand words on any subject he liked. The 1963 Hugo

Prolific and legendary science and science fiction writer Isaac Asimov is shown in 1970. Asimov was known for his visionary imagination and his ability to easily explain science to readers.

also recognized him for "introducing science into science fiction," the first of many honors.

With humble beginnings as a Jewish immigrant from Russia, Asimov told stories from an early age, publishing his first stories while in college. Among the most celebrated is the Foundation Trilogy, which would earn numerous awards and begin Asimov's journey to becoming one of the most widely read, respected, and well-paid authors of the twentieth century. In addition, Asimov had a tremendous output with the pulp magazines that became popular with audiences from the 1920s on. He expanded on some of his early ideas in novels and stories, including his equally well-known and beloved Robot novels and stories.

As a Ph.D. in chemistry, Asimov taught the subject and was immensely popular with students. But he had always been intensely curious about many different subjects. Besides writing on chemistry, physics, and astronomy, Asimov wrote hundreds of articles and dozens of books on history, culture, law, environmentalism, the Bible, literature, and much more. He made science and other topics, even difficult ones, accessible and entertaining for millions of readers. These included works as varied as *The Intelligent Man's Guide to Science*, *The Human Body*, *The Greeks: A Great Adventure*, *To the Ends of the Universe*, three volumes of *Understanding Physics*, *Great Ideas of Science*, *Asimov's Guide to the Bible*, *Asimov's Guide to Shakespeare*, and many more. Hundreds of his nonfiction articles were collected in anthologies, too. Asimov even had a humorous streak and published several books of limericks.

Regarded as the "Grand Master of Science Fiction" by peers and fans, Asimov is also credited with popularizing "hard science fiction," which attempts a more realistic imagining of humans using science and technology within imaginary worlds and universes. Asimov also incorporated ideas inspired by history, environmentalism, and humanism into his writing. Few authors were as prolific—counting anthologies of his work, Asimov published as many as 467 books.

He also popularized science and science fiction throughout the twentieth century, especially during the 1950s and 1960s, when the world's attention was focused on the space race between the United States and the Soviet Union. This is Isaac Asimov's story.

CHAPTER ONE

THE EARLY YEARS: ISAAC LOOKS TO THE STARS

One of the most prolific and beloved authors of science fiction and nonfiction of the twentieth century, Isaak Yudovich Ozimov—known to the world as Isaac Asimov—was born in 1920 in Petrovichi, Russia, then known as the Union of Soviet Socialist Republics (USSR). Because of poor record-keeping at the time, it remains unclear to this day what Asimov's date of birth was, though officially he celebrated it on January 2.

His parents, Anna Rachel Berman Asimov and Judah Asimov, then known as the Osimovs, were millers, grinding grain for bread in their village, located about 250 miles (400 kilometers) southwest of Moscow, Russia's capital. Petrovichi was in a part of Russia that was half-Jewish and half-Belarussian. Though the region had suffered anti-Jewish pogroms, or riots, Petrovichi itself had a mixed population of Jews and Christians coexisting peacefully.

Isaac would have few memories of his life in this Jewish shtetl, or village. However, his family was considered comfortable, even middle-class, by regional standards. The family took their chances and joined the wave of immigration to what they and many others considered "the Promised Land," America. It was just in the nick of time: the following year, new laws made moving to the United States much more difficult.

COMING TO AMERICA

In 1923, the Asimovs would make the long, tough trip from the Soviet Union across the Atlantic to New York City at the invitation of Isaac's uncle Joseph, his mother's brother. They had three-year-old Isaac with them, along with his younger sister, Marcia, who was only one and originally named Manya in their native land. First they traveled from Russia to Liverpool, England, where they boarded a larger ship, the *Baltic*, for the final leg of their journey.

At the time, the trip took weeks. It was unlike the quick, trans-Atlantic flights of today. The family was hopeful but nervous. Seasickness, uncomfortable conditions and bad food, and their own anxiety made the trip unpleasant. However, it marked one of Isaac's

ARRIVING A

An archival photo shows immigrants arriving on Ellis Island in New York Harbor, the gateway for most new arrivals to the United States from 1892 until 1955, including Isaac Asimov's family.

first milestones: he saw his first motion picture, or movie, on the *Baltic*.

Landing in New York City, the Asimovs passed through Ellis Island, where immigrants were processed before moving on to their final American destinations. Isaac had come down with the measles, prolonging the family's quarantine time there for several days. The Asimovs were fortunate; they already had family in New York. Isaac's uncle Joseph came to welcome them dockside.

IN EAST NEW YORK

They soon settled in the East New York section of Brooklyn, where numerous European Jews, Italians, and other immigrants resided. Like many newcomers, they had changed their family name on Ellis Island—from Osimov to Asimov.

Their first home was a ground-floor apartment on Van Siclen Avenue. Unlike their life in the village, the Asimovs were poor in America like most of their neighbors. They lacked electricity and central heating. Furthermore, they did not know English, limiting their options for employment or a livelihood.

Van Sicklen Avenue, North from Fulton Street.   BROOKLYN, N. Y.

A postcard depicts Van Siclen (formerly spelled "Sicklen") Avenue in Brooklyn's East New York around the time of the Asimovs' arrival in America. Some people recall that, as a boy, Asimov liked to read science fiction magazines in the neighboring Evergreens Cemetery.

A GIFTED CHILD

Learning English was the quickest way to assimilate, but the Asimovs spoke only Yiddish. However, young Isaac would pleasantly surprise his parents by learning to read English by teaching himself and enlisting the other neighborhood children to help him. He demonstrated an aptitude for language and learning, asking his friends how words and letters sounded and the basics of the English alphabet. Judah and Anna realized they had raised a gifted child.

The Asimovs decided not to waste any time in helping Isaac fulfill his potential. With no records proving otherwise, they told their son's school that he was slightly older than he really was, thus getting him into first grade not long after he excelled in kindergarten. At the same time, his father kept tabs on Isaac. Although he didn't prohibit him from playing with neighborhood kids, he encouraged his son to build his intellect and get as much from books as he did from the street games the world outside offered.

His parents also made sure he remained fluent in Yiddish. Although the family was technically Orthodox, they did not force religion on their son. He did not even perform the traditional rite of Jewish manhood, the bar mitzvah. This freedom would influence Isaac years later, when he declared himself nonreligious.

MOVING UP IN THE WORLD

The Asimovs moved out of their cramped apartment into a slightly larger one. Judah Asimov had become a factory worker but wanted more for his family. Scrimping and saving, the Asimovs were eventually the proud owners of their own corner candy store. Isaac's father worked long hours, and Anna Asimov covered morning shifts. The store was open from 6:00 AM until 1:00 AM every day.

Asimov later recalled in a 2002 biography, *It's Been a Good Life*, how the store saved his family from the suffering that many Americans endured during the Great Depression of the 1930s. "Well, the Asimov family escaped. Not by much. We were poor, but we always had enough to put food on the table and to pay the rent. Never were we threatened by hunger and eviction. And why? The candy store."

With his parents busy minding the store, Isaac was often alone during long stretches of the day. When he wasn't alone, he worked like everyone else instead of playing outside. He kept reading voraciously, even doing so during his meals, which he often took by himself.

His teachers soon realized his intelligence. Isaac did not need two or three times to figure out a concept, but simply absorbed nearly anything with curiosity and speed. He was the youngest student but certainly not the quietest. His only problem with discipline was that he talked in class so much. This talking was mainly because he was always so ahead of his peers that he grew bored easily. He also did not hold back from frequently declaring how smart he was, which won him few friends, he later joked.

While his father made sure he steered clear of negative influences, Isaac did have one friend who had a positive impact on his future as a writer. Solomon, nicknamed "Solly," was a storyteller, and the first one to truly introduce Isaac to telling tales, as early as the second grade. Many of the stories he and Solly ended up telling each other were ripped straight from the pulp magazines sold at the Asimovs' shop.

Later, Isaac tried out retelling tales from the pulps to fellow students. He was careful to note that he had read these, not taking credit for them himself. He later recalled, in *It's Been a Good Life*, "I discovered, for the first time that I loved to have an audience. I found that I could speak before a group, even when some of them were strangers to me, without embarrassment."

BOOKS: HIGH AND LOW

Solly moved away, but Isaac was hooked. He secretly coveted the magazines and cheap paperbacks (called

The October 1928 cover of *Amazing Stories* was typical of the artwork enjoyed by a young Isaac and countless other science fiction fans of the pulp era.

"dime novels" back then because of their price) at the candy store. He made sure to hide these obsessions from his father, who frowned upon them. When he was about to turn seven, though, his father got him a library card.

Isaac would take a long, 2-mile (3.2-km) daily walk to the library and back to borrow books, even

ISAAC'S "GREENVILLE CHUMS"

In *It's Been a Good Life*, Asimov talked about his earliest writing attempts. Just before turning twelve, Isaac started "The Greenville Chums at College," based on a book he read, *The Darewell Chums at College*. He tried out the first two chapters on a friend, Emmanuel Bershadsky, during lunch one day.

To Isaac's surprise, Emmanuel asked, "Can I borrow the book when you've finished reading it?" His friend had naturally assumed Isaac was again retelling a tale he had read elsewhere. From then on, Isaac began to take himself seriously as a writer and storyteller. Although he gave up on it after about eight chapters, it was still an impressive effort for a middle school student.

reading on the way. Although he felt stifled by the two-book-per-visit limit, he worked around this by getting the longest books possible. He loved Charles Dickens's *Pickwick Papers*, which he claimed he read twenty-five times.

Later, Isaac read more adult literature and non-fiction. Still, he loved the anthology magazines *Astounding* and *Amazing Stories*. He also devoured adventure tales, Westerns, and other exciting subject matter. With his father and mother working the same tough hours at the store, and expecting a new baby, Isaac indulged his passions for science fiction and fantasy. Reading these was formative for one of the future overlords of science fiction and science nonfiction in the twentieth century.

UPS AND DOWNS

Isaac entered Boys High School of Brooklyn early. He was only twelve, and most of his peers were fifteen. Around that time, the family moved to Ridgewood, a neighborhood in the borough of Queens, bordering Brooklyn. Many of the neighbors were German and the area was heavily Catholic. For the first time, Isaac felt slightly excluded because he was Jewish. The Asimovs were not devout at all, but he still felt how he and his family were in the minority.

This photograph depicts the original site of Boys High School, the oldest public high school in Brooklyn, New York, where Isaac spent part of his teenage years.

Because Isaac still absorbed almost all of his lessons and readings so quickly, he often grew bored. Still, there were many boys in his school far ahead of him, and he could no longer count on being in the very top of his class. His father still pressed him to do his best, so Isaac had to explain himself whenever he fell short of perfect grades.

Isaac yearned to share his stories more widely. At fourteen, he took a chance when his teacher, Mr. Newfield, assigned a descriptive essay. Describing a country morning in the spring, Isaac read it aloud in class. He had been reading a great deal of nineteenth-century literature at the time, and the essay was filled with flowery language about birds and the natural world.

Unfortunately, his teacher hated it and expressed so to the class, according to Michael White's biography, *Isaac Asimov: A Life of the Grand Master of Science Fiction*. Isaac refused to be discouraged. He continued writing and bounced back with a humor piece called "Little Brothers," a contribution to the school magazine, later also reprinted in his school's literary journal, *The Boys High Recorder*.

In 1935, Isaac would receive the most important tool of his trade, a gift from his father: a used Underwood typewriter. Typing lessons were soon arranged with a young neighbor girl, Mazie. Though she offered regular lessons, as Asimov related in *It's Been a Good Life*, "[I] had my pride. No one was ever allowed to teach me any more than I required to begin teaching myself. 'That's all right,' I said. 'I'll practice.'" Eventually, he mastered typing, achieving ninety words per minute. He burned through forty pages of a fantasy story populated with dwarves, sword fights, and wizards. He soon realized, however, that his true passion was science fiction, not fantasy.

CHAPTER TWO

FROM FAN TO WRITER

J ust as he had advanced through the earlier grades, Isaac Asimov was ready to graduate high school at the tender age of fifteen. His parents wanted him to be a doctor, a well-paid and respected profession. It was decided that Isaac would apply to Seth Low College, an affiliate of Columbia University's Columbia College that accepted mainly students from immigrant backgrounds, including Jews, Italians, and others. At the time, quotas controlled how many students of Jewish background could attend Columbia itself, and qualified, accepted applicants beyond the quota typically went to Seth Low.

His family moved near Brooklyn's Prospect Park onto Windsor Place, where Isaac's writing truly took off. He had his own room and now had permission from his father, and enough space, to store his copies of *Amazing Stories* and *Astounding Science Fiction*. He even recalled the exact date he started writing seriously: May 29, 1937. It was then that he began a story about time travel, "Cosmic Corkscrew," basing it on where he thought modern-day science might soon go.

ASIMOV: PROFESSIONAL FAN

The community of science fiction fans at the time was very active. Asimov was among the frequent contributors writing letters to the editor, often praising, critiquing, and rating the published stories and articles according to his own criteria. He even received letters back from some authors.

He also joined a community of science fiction fans in New York. Short for "fanatics," fans were the readers who lived and breathed science fiction. Clubs existed all over the United States, their members obsessing over the pulps. Asimov was now eighteen, and aside from his college classes and his job at the store, his trips across the city were opportunities to talk about the genre and make new friends.

Asimov first joined the Greater New York Science Fiction Club, a group of young fans based in Queens. They discussed stories, read their own work, and gossiped about other clubs. The clubs often split up and reformed after intense arguments. He soon joined one of the most important clubs, the Futurians. Some of the most prominent twentieth-century science fiction writers were members and would befriend Asimov, including Robert Heinlein and Frederik Pohl.

AN *ASTOUNDING* STEP

One month, Asimov visited *Astounding*'s offices. Like the letters he received from authors, this visit bridged the distance in his mind between Asimov and his heroes, the writers who filled its pages, and even the editorial staff. He later recalled, in *It's Been a Good Life*, that the *Astounding* office "existed in a real building in a real space, a building I could reach and enter and it contained people who would speak to me." He decided to get serious and rework "Cosmic Corkscrew" for submission.

The thrifty nature he had inherited from his father, plus Judah's own advice for his son, led to a discussion on how best to submit the story. It was one of the first times he had spoken directly with Judah about his writing. Together, thy calculated that taking the subway there and back would be two cents cheaper than mailing it in. Judah advised him to turn in the manuscript personally to John Campbell, the editor.

It was a nerve-wracking trip to the offices. But Asimov gathered his courage, went up to the receptionist, and asked to see the editor. After a quick phone call, she surprised the young man by saying that Campbell would see him.

Campbell was a respected and prolific science fiction author at the time. Although Asimov

A STREET AND SMITH PUBLICATION

Astounding

SCIENCE FICTION

BRITISH
9ᴰ.
EDITION

MARCH

THE CURRENTS OF SPACE *BY* ISAAC ASIMOV

John Campbell, the editor of *Astounding Science Fiction*, developed high standards in science fiction writing that became known as its golden age. The first installment of Asimov's novel *The Currents of Space* made the cover of the March 1953 issue.

was amazed that he could simply show up unannounced and obtain a meeting so easily, Campbell loved to talk and was always curious about and eager to hire new talent. He took the young man's story and promised to read it and send a letter informing Asimov whether it had been accepted or rejected.

That first encounter with Campbell, then only twenty-eight years old, proved crucial for Asimov. Campbell was one of the most influential figures in science fiction. He was responsible for moving the genre from childish, action-oriented pulp fiction to the "hard science fiction" that Asimov would soon begin to write.

ASIMOV THE UNDERGRAD

Asimov's higher-education career was as colorful and complicated as his time in high school. He perhaps had more passion for writing than he did for his classes, even though he excelled at his studies. With his humor and sarcasm, he annoyed his college professors occasionally, much as he had his high school instructors. His constant joking almost got Asimov kicked out of two different classes. Only his intelligence and good grades saved him from disciplinary action.

In addition, there was early proof that Asimov was not cut out for practical science or medicine. In one biology class, students had to catch a stray cat to kill, preserve, and dissect it. Asimov forced himself to do it and soon dropped out of the zoology major he had picked, entering the chemistry program instead.

Before Asimov's sophomore year, Seth Low closed. Its students were packed off to Columbia University. The long commute to upper Manhattan from Brooklyn and his commitment to helping out at the candy store made a social life at Columbia difficult. As he became serious about writing professionally—especially to earn money to pay tuition—it was even more impressive that Asimov was able to meet his academic requirements.

GRAD SCHOOL: A CHANGE OF PLANS

Finishing his undergraduate studies proved to be just as rocky for Asimov. Against the odds, he completed a bachelor of science in chemistry in 1939. Despite his parents' hopes that he would become a doctor, it was not to be. He applied to five different medical schools and was rejected by all of them.

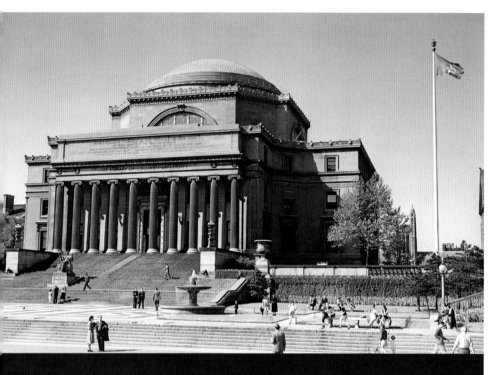

The Low Memorial Library of Columbia University, Asimov's alma mater, is shown here in an archival photo.

In September 1939, just as World War II was breaking out in Europe, Asimov entered the graduate program in chemistry at Columbia. His troublemaking reputation followed him, and he angered several professors. One teacher, Professor Urey, even voted against allowing Asimov to continue as a graduate but was outvoted by his peers on the selection committee.

Asimov loved learning and science, but he would continue an uncertain path to a traditional career as a scientist or academic. Meanwhile, his true passion was just getting off the ground. Shortly after the meeting with Campbell, his writing career would take him on a lifelong journey to the stars and beyond.

REJECTIONS PILE UP

Within two days of meeting Campbell, Asimov received the big news via mail: Campbell had rejected "Cosmic Corkscrew." Rather than discouraging him, however, Campbell's detailed criticisms helped. Campbell disliked the first-person narration, the story's slow start, and the length, which was "too long for a short story, too short for a novelette," at nine thousand words.

According to Asimov, the polite suggestions and the promising meeting with the editor himself inspired him. "I was off and running," he later wrote. Campbell "filled me with the ambition to write another science fiction story, one that was better than the first." He even began imagining a new story on his way home from meeting Campbell, called "Stowaway." He wrote it, keeping it to six thousand words. It, too, was rejected. But once again, the editor energized Asimov with a helpful rejection letter.

"HARD SCIENCE FICTION"

John Campbell, Isaac Asimov, and other writers whom Campbell helped groom at *Astounding* marked a shift in the science fiction of their era. The old stories from pulps—with their fast-paced action, outlandish characters, spacemen and ray guns, and other cartoonish elements—were on the way out. Taking their place was the "hard science fiction" that Asimov and his peers would make popular. This style focused more on thoughtful characters, big concepts, and more realistic situations at least somewhat based on science itself. Authors concentrated on creating worlds that might exist one day. Fantastic phenomena, such as space flight, were explained using science. Fans and critics would later call this era science fiction's golden age.

PUBLICATION: THREE ASIMOV MILESTONES

Armed with a new Smith-Corona typewriter purchased by his father, who saw how serious Asimov was about being a writer, he got to work. He even learned from his correspondence with other authors. Cliff Simak, who had a story in *Astounding*'s July 1938 issue, asked for more feedback from Asimov, who had critiqued the story in a letter to the magazine. Letters back and forth with him inspired Asimov to rethink his criticisms and incorporate a smoother writing style more like Simak's. He eliminated unnecessary transitions between scenes, for example. It paid off: Asimov's writing became tighter and more focused.

Over the following months, Asimov submitted five stories to Campbell. All were rejected. On October 21, four months to the day that he first met Campbell, *Amazing Stories* accepted "Marooned Off Vesta" and "The Weapon Too Dreadful to Use" for its March and May 1939 issues, respectively. It would be months until Campbell accepted his story "Trends" for July 1939 publication in *Astounding*.

"Trends," in particular, typified the more serious science fiction that Campbell and Asimov focused on. Originally titled "Ad Astra," (after the Latin proverb "*Per aspera ad astra*," or "Through difficulties to the stars") the story was inspired by his research duties for Columbia sociology professor Bernard J. Stern. Stern was doing a book on society's opposition to technological advances, and Asimov thought it would make a good theme for a story. In "Trends," there is opposition to space travel in mankind's quest to land on the moon, an event still thirty years in the future in 1939.

however, and it was later included in dictionaries and became the term that scientists and laypeople used.

Another influential aspect of his robot stories was a system of laws governing robot behavior. Called "The Three Laws of Robotics," they would appear in Asimov's short works and his later robot novels. They would even influence many other science fiction writers and filmmakers. The Three Laws of Robotics are as follows:

1. A robot may not injure a human being or, through inaction, allow a human being to come to harm.
2. A robot must obey the orders given it by human beings except where such orders would conflict with the First Law.
3. A robot must protect its own existence as long as such protection does not conflict with the First or Second Laws.

These rules also introduced a new way for Asimov and later storytellers to portray robots. Earlier fictional robots often turned against their creators. Asimov realized this story line had been used hundreds of times before and vowed never to use it himself.

A FOUNDATION FOR A WRITER'S LIFE

I n 1941, John Campbell, referencing a work by Ralph Waldo Emerson, asked his protégé to write a story about people who witness the first appearance of stars in the sky in a thousand years. The resulting tale, "Nightfall," would become one of Asimov's most acclaimed and well-regarded stories. Campbell liked it so much that he paid the author more per word than for any of his past submissions.

THE BEGINNINGS OF THE FOUNDATION SAGA

Asimov always loved historical novels. In 1941, he decided to write a future history, with his main inspiration the eighteenth-century text by Edward Gibbon, *The History of the Decline and Fall of the Roman Empire.* He imagined the fall of a Galactic Empire, written from the point of view of someone living

FIRST LOVE: GERTRUDE BLUGERMAN

In early 1942, Asimov met Gertrude Blugerman. Gertrude's friend Lee was dating Asimov's friend Joe, a fellow member of the Brooklyn Authors Club. Asimov was not a ladies' man upon first glance; he was, as biographer Michael White described him, "an odd mix of introvert [meaning shy] and loudmouth." He had strong opinions, was thrifty with his money, and had rough social skills. However, he could be both charming and witty when he wanted to be. He and Gertrude hit it off and began dating.

Gertrude grew up in Canada and had moved to New York with her family at age nineteen. They had been dating only a few months before Asimov proposed to her. Despite initially saying no, he was persistent and persuasive, and she eventually agreed to marry him. (They were married during the summer.)

during the Second Galactic Empire. In *It's Been a Good Life*, he said he planned a "science fiction story that *read* like a historical novel."

He approached John Campbell, who quickly agreed that the story was too big for a simple short story. Campbell seemed even more excited about the idea than Asimov was. He soon pressed the author for an outline detailing this future history, an idea inspired by a project that science fiction author Robert Heinlein was then writing, his Future History series.

Asimov soon became anxious. He hated outlining projects, and his first attempt at plotting out the story confirmed this. He later wrote in *I, Asimov*, "I went home, dutifully, and began preparing an outline that got longer and longer, and stupider and stupider until I finally tore it up."

Instead, he stuck to his original idea. In the first story, "Foundation," first published in *Astounding*'s May 1942 issue, the First Galactic Empire is beginning to fall apart. The characters discover a plan set decades before to establish a central location for knowledge and culture to survive the empire's fall. This plan would also help minimize the time of galactic chaos from a predicted thirty thousand years to just a thousand. As Michael White noted in his biography of the author, Asimov was perhaps "the first pulp writer to create a hero who was not a ray-gun-toting superhero, but a middle-aged politician," referring to Salvor Hardin, the first story's protagonist.

He followed up with "Bridle and Saddle." This second story stumped him—it was one of the few times that Asimov suffered writer's block. Fellow author Frederik Pohl was briefly Asimov's literary agent then. They took a walk over the Brooklyn Bridge to work out plot snags. Asimov submitted it in November 1941.

While the responsibilities of the war years greatly lowered Asimov's output, he wrote several more stories about the Foundation. "The Big and the Little," later called "The Merchant Princes," appeared in 1944, along with the fourth installment, "The Wedge." A fifth, "Dead Hand," followed the same year. The next part, called "The Mule," was his most sophisticated installment yet. It would also be the last visit. These stories, along with those he wrote in the coming decade, would later comprise his most famous work, the Foundation series.

THE PHILADELPHIA NAVY YARD YEARS

His academic career just beginning, Asimov received an offer he could not refuse. Through John Campbell, he met fellow author and scientist Robert Heinlein. Decades later, along with Arthur C. Clarke, Asimov and Heinlein would be the known as "the Big Three" of science fiction of the twentieth century.

At this time, Heinlein was a U.S. Navy veteran and scientist, like Asimov, and they became friends. In early 1942, Heinlein offered Asimov a job as a

A wartime photograph shows close friends and science fiction legends *(from left to right)* Robert Heinlein, Sprague de Camp, and Asimov at the Philadelphia Navy Yard.

chemist with the Philadelphia Naval Shipyard. A real salary for his first real job was tempting. Asimov accepted because, aside from an uncertain writing career, he needed stability and money. He and Gertrude were about to get married.

Asimov's Ph.D. in chemistry would have to wait. He was now a chemist at the Navy Yard. His work concentrated on paints used in camouflage,

Showing his well-known playful side, Asimov mugs for the camera while embracing his first wife, Gertrude Blugerman, with whom Asimov would start a family.

explosives, food for the troops, and battlefield phar-
maceuticals. Heinlein was an aeronautical engineer
and did not work alongside Asimov, but the two often
socialized and lunched together. After he proposed
to Gertrude, Asimov spent his weekends off travel-
ing to New York to visit her. They were married at her
family's Brooklyn home on July 26, 1942, in a small
private ceremony.

The newlyweds settled down once Gertrude moved
to Philadelphia to join her husband. All the while,
however, Asimov feared that he might be drafted. His
poor vision and his work as a wartime chemist had
given him a 2B rating when World War II began, making it unlikely, however. Although he did not welcome
the idea of fighting and felt that he would probably
make a terrible soldier, Asimov mainly feared being
overseas away from his wife and family. He was
proud, however, that he did his part in the scientific
field to further the war effort.

IN THE ARMY

Ironically, the war ended in Europe in May 1945,
and the Japanese surrendered in August 1945 after
the atomic bombs fell on Hiroshima and Nagasaki.
Asimov was a few months away from turning twenty-
six, the age he would become ineligible for the draft.

Because his exact birthday had never been determined, his mother had it established as January 2 back in the third grade. Had they picked an earlier date (his birthdate may have been as early as September 1919), he may have escaped the draft.

Instead, he received a new 1AB rating, making him eligible. He wanted to go back to Columbia but realized how lucky he was when so many Americans and others had given life and limb in combat. Asimov was drafted and shipped off to Fort Meade, Maryland, and later to basic training.

The science fiction writer and academic soon realized that he would never make an ideal soldier. One officer declared sadly that he "didn't know his left foot from his right." He was often lonely and made few friends. Wisely, he limited his usual wisecracks and misbehavior that had bothered countless teachers throughout his school career.

Still, he was spared from the harsher duties of an army private because of his intelligence and superior typing ability. Though he only learned of it much later, he scored extremely high on the army's equivalent of an I.Q. test, the Army General Classification Test (AGCT). His 160 score actually made his superiors decide that they should not waste time in trying to make him a soldier but rather ignore him.

Basic training was uncomfortable for Asimov because of the physical challenges. He made it through by writing letters, and he enjoyed the base's library. It was there that he discovered a military order that declared that research chemists could apply for early release. His hopes up, he found army life more bearable. Knowing that typists were always in demand, Asimov also cleverly revealed his abilities to a superior officer and became the camp typist, thus avoiding other tougher duties.

OPERATION CROSSROADS... AND DISCHARGE

Intelligence did not always work in Asimov's favor. His high AGCT score was the main reason why he was picked as a specialist for a secret project. By March 1946, Asimov was headed to Hawaii. The men soon discovered that they were part of Operation Crossroads. Asimov and other scientists were to be shipped thousands of miles to Bikini Atoll in the western Pacific Ocean. There, the United States would explode the first atomic bomb since World War II ended and analyze its effects.

Soon, however, he received word from Gertrude in New York that the army had withheld a monthly military support payment because Asimov was to be discharged. Eventually, he got to the bottom of things, thanks to a commanding officer. The officer asked him if he indeed had applied for a discharge.

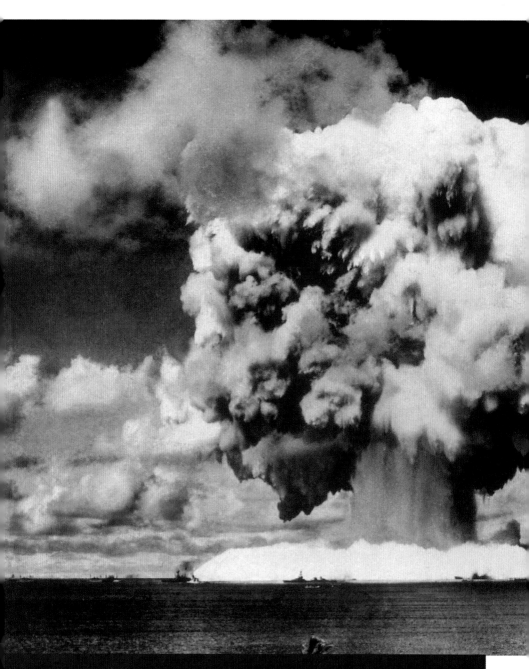

Shown here is the first atomic bomb test at Bikini Atoll in the Pacific Ocean on July 1, 1946, the first of a series of bombs tested by the United States.

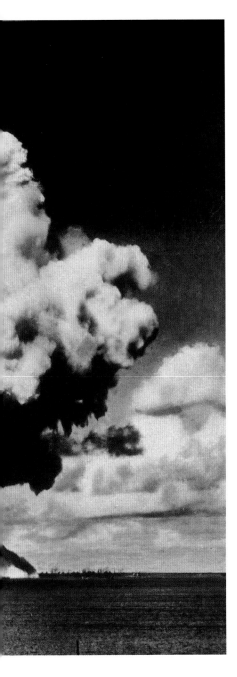

Asimov had, earlier that February. Despite suspecting that it was a mistake, the officer told him it was against the policy of the operation to include anyone who might be discharged.

Soon, he was off the project, and he left Hawaii mere days before the other specialists sailed for Bikini Atoll. For a scientist, it may have been a once-in-a-lifetime opportunity to work on a nuclear project. However, Asimov also mused later, "It also meant that, perhaps, I did not die of leukemia at a comparatively early age." After admitting at his discharge hearing that he did not think he could cut it as a soldier or an officer, Asimov was discharged. Miraculously, he was on his way home.

CHAPTER FOUR

THE FALL AND RISE OF DR. ASIMOV

I n the postwar years, John Campbell pressed Isaac
Asimov for more Foundation material. Asimov
wanted to explore other territory, including more
robot stories, and start writing a novel. Still, he deliv-
ered another Foundation story called "Now You See
It" in February 1947. It included a definite ending,
but Campbell wanted more. Asimov changed it, and
"Now You Don't" followed in March 1949. Asimov
had decided that he was finished with the series.

In the army, he only wrote the robot story
"Evidence." As of September 1946, he was twenty-
seven years old and enrolled again at Columbia
University. He had to review much of the current
research in his field and hurriedly catch up on new
developments.

One crucial milestone remained. To finish his
Ph.D. and gain the title of doctor, Asimov had to turn
in his dissertation and pass his oral exams. He was

Asimov is shown in his younger and more clean-cut days, sometime before he adopted the sideburns that would become his trademark.

extremely nervous because he had a reputation for being unorthodox and a bit of a troublemaker. With some anxiety, and some nervous laughter throughout, Asimov braved the examination. At the end, when the doctoral panel came out, he was relieved and overjoyed to hear their decision. "Congratulations, Dr. Asimov!" they said.

OFF TO BOSTON

Asimov loved New York but soon faced a difficult choice. His career at Columbia was uninspiring, and he felt insecure in his position there. He started shopping around for other jobs and grew anxious about his lack of leads. He was relieved when Billy Boyd called him from the Boston University School of Medicine (BUSM).

Boyd offered Asimov a yearlong instructorship at BUSM, although without any guarantees about future employment or possibilities for promotion. It was not enough to quit Columbia and uproot the Asimovs. He turned it down.

BUSM persisted, offering him more money and a one-month, annual paid vacation. He began a series of interviews. Dr. Burnham S. Walker, Boyd's boss, who had liked Asimov's doctoral dissertation, told him part of the job would be teaching freshmen at the medical school, including biochemistry. Asimov agreed, even though he knew he had to brush up on the subject.

In April 1949, he received the formal appointment in the mail that he could officially start as an instructor in biochemistry as of May 1. After two months of scrambling for work, Asimov realized he was ready to move on. Growing up in the Depression, he did not dare count on his writing to guarantee him and Gertrude a steady income. He would be proved wrong down the line, of course.

A NOVEL APPROACH

In 1950, Doubleday published Asimov's first novel, *Pebble in the Sky*. It featured a time-traveling tailor from the twentieth century as the hero. Much of Earth had become radioactive from nuclear conflict and is considered a rebellious planet. Asimov tied racism, fanaticism, and oppression into a story set in a world where the elderly are euthanized at age sixty.

Asimov began the story, formerly titled "Grow Old with Me," in 1947 at the urging of *Thrilling Wonder* editor Sam Merwin. Merwin wanted to publish it as a forty-thousand-word novel, the lead piece in a related magazine, *Startling Stories*. The novel reflected the fear of nuclear war that dominated the 1950s, as the

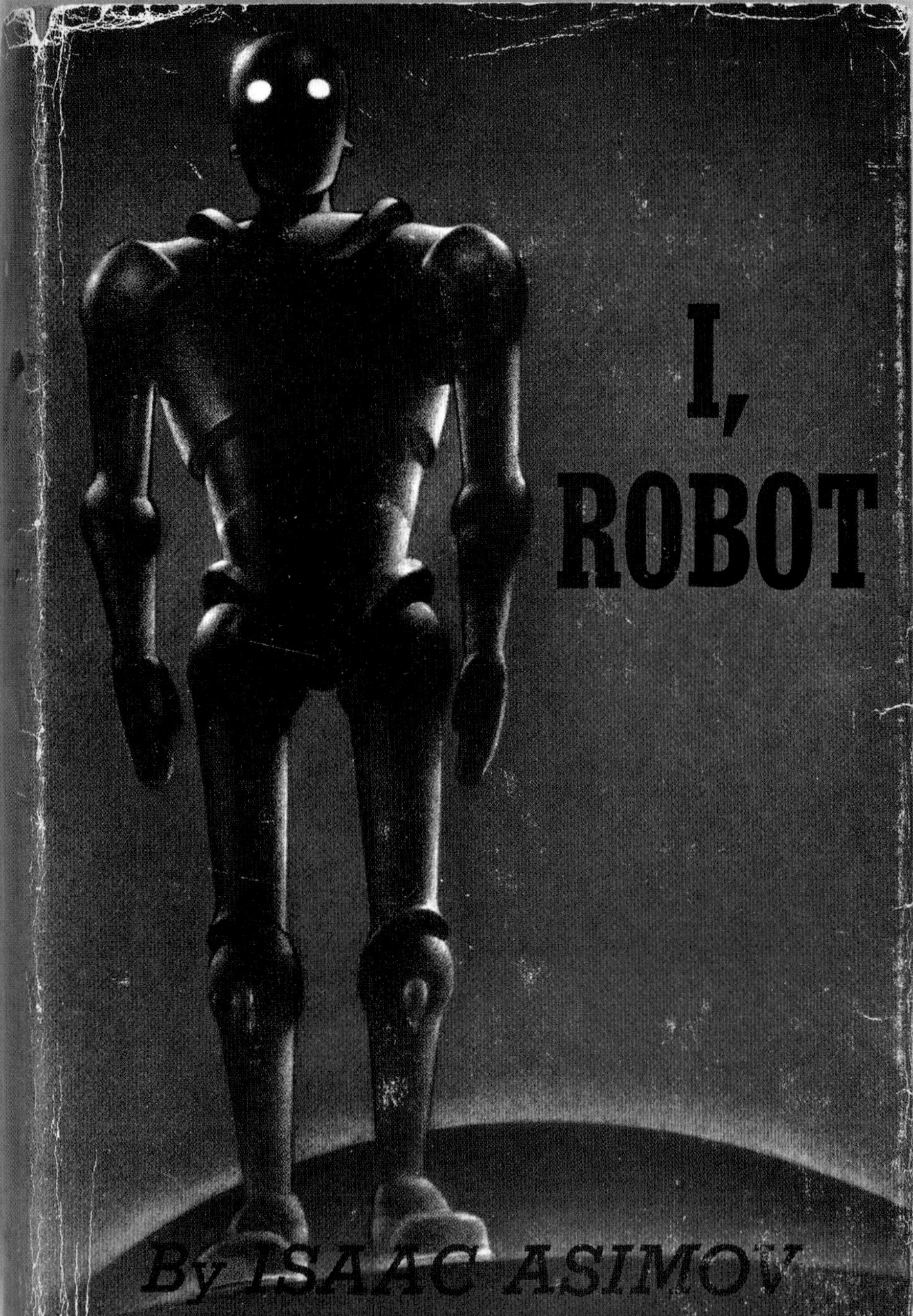

I,
ROBOT

By ISAAC ASIMOV

The first edition dust jacket cover of the *I, Robot* anthology of short stories, published by Gnome Press in 1950, is shown here, as illustrated by Edd Cartier.

United States and the Soviet Union raced to develop ever more weapons. It also marked the first of several works that would take place in a unified, consistent reality, the Galactic Empire of the Foundation stories.

The Foundation saga did not disappear either. Frederik Pohl contacted Martin Greenberg, who managed Gnome Press, to put out Asimov's material

THE ASIMOVS: A NEW GENERATION

Isaac and Gertrude Asimov were glad for the financial stability that Isaac's academic post and his burgeoning writing career offered because they would soon start a family. On August 20, 1951, David Asimov entered the world. Asimov wrote that he had expected David to be their only child, especially because Gertrude was already thirty-four at his birth. However, a few years later, on February 19, 1955, Gertrude gave birth to the Asimovs' second child, Robyn Joan. Isaac insisted they spell her name with a "y" to prevent anyone from thinking she was a boy and that her middle name was an alternative in case she disliked her first name later in life.

in a longer format. Greenberg's Asimov releases would include not only reworked versions of the Foundation material but also a volume of nine of the author's robot stories written between 1939 and 1950. The collection was entitled *I, Robot* and released in 1950.

THE FOUNDATION TRILOGY

Gnome Press resurrected the Foundation stories to even greater success and acclaim. With an extra section written to introduce the setting to readers ("The Pyschohistorians"), it published the entire series as a trilogy of novels. *Foundation* (1951), *Foundation and Empire* (1952), and *Second Foundation* (1953) would eventually make Asimov a household name and perhaps the most successful science fiction author of his era.

Numerous critics and millions of fans have praised the series, and it inspired the careers of many writers, plus countless novels, films, and television series. Asimov himself admitted surprise when, at the twenty-fourth World Science Fiction Convention in 1966, it won the Hugo Award for Best All-Time Series, beating out works like J. R. R. Tolkien's The

The covers of the Foundation trilogy from the series' 1973 edition are depicted, one of many reprints over the years.

Lord of the Rings trilogy and Robert Heinlein's Future History series.

THE ROBOT NOVELS

Building on his Three Laws of Robotics, Asimov penned two full-length robot novels in the 1950s. *The Caves of Steel* (1954) was science fiction that incorporated strong elements of a mystery and detective novel. It paired a human and a robot as a detective team solving a murder. In the story, Earth is overpopulated and dominated by a rich elite living in huge, domed cities, from which the book gets its title. Critics praised what they saw as a criticism of technology, bureaucracy, and a world lacking enough resources, as well as the clever combination of science fiction and crime novel. This detective duo returns in Asimov's sequel, *The Naked Sun* (1957), which also depicts how robots might behave, and portrays an alien society (the Solarians) where people avoid all contact with each other, living in isolation.

AT BUSM: A ROCKY RELATIONSHIP

Asimov's independent spirit and outside writing seemed to cause as much trouble at his new workplace as some of the political struggles that he depicted in his Foundation works. He worried about how his writing career might conflict with his academic duties. The jacket flap author biography for *Pebble in the Sky* mentioned his cancer research at BUSM, even though he had never discussed the bio with the publishers. He feared a negative reaction from the administration.

Asimov sought out Dean Faulkner to ask him if he should resign for possibly providing the school with unwanted or negative publicity. The dean only asked him if it was a good book, and Asimov answered that the publishers thought so. This seemed to satisfy Faulkner, who said the medical school would be glad to be identified with it.

This one reassuring event did not prevent other friction between Asimov and his superiors, however. Resentment grew between the two, and between Asimov and some of his fellow faculty, for several reasons. In *It's Been a Good Life*, he wrote, "My history, well into middle age, was marked by my inability to get along with my fellows and my superiors."

One reason that Asimov mentioned in several autobiographies was professional jealousy. As a researcher and practical chemist, he admitted that he was mediocre. But his growing fame as a science fiction writer spread and was well known to his faculty peers. Some were even fans—others, not so much.

Some of this resentment was because of Asimov's income. Throughout the 1950s, he began earning more money from his stories and novels than even some of the accomplished, tenured professors and administrators. He also had his modest academic salary. "I tried to make up for my outside income by never asking for a raise," Asimov said. This backfired when it came to his treatment by BUSM's administration because it "was interpreted as meaning that that was all I deserved," he wrote in *It's Been a Good Life*.

His reputation as a favorite lecturer among students may have also caused problems with some jealous colleagues. Many of his peers dealt with very serious and complicated concepts, and their lectures were nowhere near as fun-filled and exciting as Asimov's introductory courses.

Other peers and superiors disliked Asimov because, as he related in *I, Asimov*, he eventually "gave up any pretense of doing research." He preferred teaching and writing books. His biochemistry work suffered setbacks. His colleagues Bill Boyd and Burnham Walker pitched in with Asimov to write *Biochemistry and Human Metabolism* in May 1952. Their book competed against two other similar texts released simultaneously, and their book sold poorly.

SHOWDOWN

One researcher was angered by Asimov's stubbornness in not doing laboratory work and made life hard for the wisecracking, eccentric junior professor. Dr. Henry Lemon was conservative, thorough, dedicated to research, and not a popular instructor with students—in other words, everything Asimov was not. Lemon thought the science fiction writer's presence on the faculty was undignified and embarrassing to BUSM. He found an ally in Dr. Charles Keefer, who also felt no great love for Asimov. Keefer was one step higher than Walker, Asimov's own boss.

Despite all this, Asimov continued to do less research and more teaching at the university. Some faculty and members of the administration were on his side. They saw having a celebrated author on staff as good publicity for the school. Asimov eventually received tenure, a permanent position with a university that includes strong job security. In 1955, he had finally become an associate professor in chemistry. His days at the school were numbered, however.

Walker was later replaced with another administrator who had little idea of the political struggle taking place around him. Asimov's critics started playing hardball. They tried to force him to do research. He responded forcefully that he could be very useful to the school as a science writer and instructor, but that he was "simply mediocre" as a researcher. Asimov insisted it would be a waste of their time and his to force the issue.

In response, his enemies forced the university to make an ultimatum: unless Asimov resumed research, he would be fired by the end of June 1958. They pointed out that the school could not afford to pay someone to simply write about science. Asimov attempted (cleverly, he thought) to continue on unpaid. He would stop teaching, however. But he would not budge on his title and tenure, which he meant to keep at all cost. He thought the university would avoid the bad publicity of forcing him out and that pushing him out was unethical and illegal under the terms of his tenure. Asimov almost took the matter to court.

Luckily, the university backed down. Asimov kept his tenure and title, but the 1957–1958 academic year was his last with BUSM. He had bigger fish to fry, anyway. His fame as a science fiction writer, and a new focus on nonfiction, would soon make him a household name in popular science.

ALL'S WELL THAT END'S WELL

In the end, everything worked out in Asimov's favor. He later admitted that even if he wanted to remain on staff at BUSM, he would have had to sacrifice his true calling: writing full-time. Even as a prolific author of science fiction stories and novels, he had not fully considered writing his life's work until recently. He had even enforced a strict rule of no science fiction writing on campus because he thought it unethical to do so on the school's time. By the time he was about to finish his university duties, he was making five times more from his books than he did in academia.

On his first day as a full-time writer, Asimov went right to work. He started *The Clock We Live On*, which covered astronomy and chronometry, the study of timekeeping. Rather than let his anxiety consume him, he approached the topics confidently. His science background, a lifetime of reading, and even science fiction books had given him a good grasp on many things beyond just chemistry. His incredible recall helped, too; Asimov said he could remember almost every fact or bit of trivia he had ever read.

THE WRITING PROCESS

Asimov claimed that he did all his own typing and research and answered all his own mail. Except for briefly hiring his friend Frederik Pohl to represent him very early on, Asimov never had an agent. Besides

Asimov used an old-fashioned Underwood typewriter for much of his career, then switched to a Smith-Corona, and only later in life did he adopt electronic means to put his ideas on the page.

switching from a manual typewriter to an electric one, and later to a word processor toward the end of his life, he adopted few other new technologies, especially not for the nuts and bolts of his writing.

His work ethic was legendary, especially when he started writing full-time. When he sat down for a day's work, it often lasted from 7:30 AM until 10 PM. He claimed that he never needed an alarm clock because he always woke up at 6 AM daily.

Asimov also very rarely did more than two drafts of a text. Usually, the first draft of a manuscript was very close to the published version. Asimov estimated that he would change about 5 percent of any given text. This quick turnaround was one reason he was able to put out so many books in a short period of time.

CHAPTER FIVE

THE GREAT EXPLAINER: ASIMOV AND NONFICTION

E arly on as a lecturer, Asimov gained a reputation for making dozens of different and sometimes difficult subjects clear and entertaining. In 1948, for example, his friends the Segals visited and asked him to explain his Columbia research. Asimov used his hands and fingers to show various chemical formulas and explained antimalarial chemicals and their reactions. As Asimov wrote in *It's Been a Good Life*, when he finished, Jack Segal told Asimov, "You're a very good explainer. I wouldn't have thought anyone could have made that clear to me." He was also called "the great explainer of our age" both by his friend the scientist and writer Carl Sagan and by journalist Bill Moyers.

STEPPING AWAY FROM FICTION

Asimov's transition from fiction to nonfiction was helped along by several factors, some within his own

According to Asimov's autobiography *In Joy Still Felt*, the astronomer and author Carl Sagan, shown here in 1970, was one of the few people Asimov considered smarter than himself.

life and others because of shifts in the larger culture. Even for such a famously hardworking author, his prolific output began to take its toll. He knew he was losing steam and that his heart was not in it like it used to be. The more he wrote on scientific subjects and other things that were not make-believe, the more he thrilled at the possibilities.

THE NEW WAVE OF SCIENCE FICTION

The hard science fiction that Asimov, his editors, and his peers had pioneered during the 1940s and 1950s began to decline. A new era was beginning, with new writers who explored different subjects and styles. The old stories of space travel, robots, and other themes with a harder scientific foundation felt old-fashioned.

Asimov followed new authors' work and still faithfully attended science fiction conventions. He wrote very little science fiction during this era, however. In one autobiography, *In Joy Still Felt*, he wrote of how science fiction had moved on and he felt no desire to change with the times: "I felt that I didn't measure up any longer and I didn't want to prove it." He was always proud of his work in the genre, but deep down he also feared being considered "just a science fiction writer."

THE SPACE RACE AND A NEW MARKET

Another reason Asimov was able to so easily jump into nonfiction was the public hunger for science texts and information. On October 4, 1957, the Soviet Union launched the first artificial Earth satellite, *Sputnik 1*, shocking the United States and beginning the competition known as the Space Race, in which both nations competed for superiority in space exploration. American society raced to catch

A Soviet technician adjusts the *Sputnik 1* satellite in 1957, the launch of which would shock the United States.

up to the Soviets via education reforms, and everyday citizens hungered for information, including books, on scientific phenomena. Asimov felt a responsibility to use science to educate the public.

FIRST NONFICTION FORAYS: THE 1950S

Asimov collaborated on 1952's *Biochemistry and Human Metabolism*, an academic text, with fellow authors William Boyd and Burnham Walker. However, it was writing for a nonacademic readership that would truly fulfill him.

In February 1955, Asimov sold his first-ever science essay. Based on a longer article that he had written for the *Journal of Chemical Education*, "Hemoglobin and the Universe" was aimed at laypeople. In *I, Asimov*, the author explained how he wanted "to make it longer, more informal, more jovial," also describing in *It's Been a Good Life* how much he enjoyed explaining the facts in a "friendly, bouncy...and personal way."

Astounding printed science articles for science fiction fans and published it in February 1955. For Asimov, the experience was eye opening: "It opened the floodgates, for from then on, I was eager to write essays on science," he wrote in *I, Asimov*. It was a style of writing that fit him like a glove.

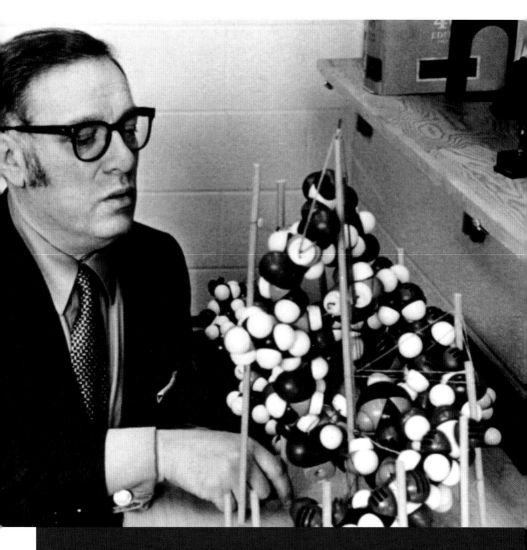

Asimov is shown here sometime around the early 1970s handling a molecular model.

Asimov published several more introductory science titles during the 1950s, even as he continued publishing mostly science fiction. These included an overview of nuclear physics, *Inside the Atom*, in 1956 and *The Building Blocks of the Universe* in 1957. In the latter, he introduced the elements of the periodic table and gave concrete, everyday examples of their properties. Critics and readers have praised the book for giving novice readers an appreciation for how chemistry works, especially many young readers tackling chemistry in middle and high school.

THE INTELLIGENT MAN'S GUIDE TO SCIENCE

In 1959, Basic Books editor Leon Svirsky asked Asimov for a general overview of the sciences for a mass audience. Asimov was anxious about accepting such an ambitious project. After holding out, it was his friend Janet Jeppson who encouraged him. He met Jeppson at a science fiction convention in New York in 1956, and they ran into each other two years later and became close. Jeppson insisted that he could and should do the book, and he signed the contract in July 1959.

Svirsky came up with a title, *The Intelligent Man's Guide to Science*, referencing *The Intelligent Woman's Guide to Socialism and Capitalism*, an earlier work by George Bernard Shaw, the respected Irish playwright and economist. Asimov thought the title would turn off potential readers, but Svirsky remained firm. Feminists later criticized Asimov for it, but he countered that the intelligent man referred to Asimov himself and not the target audience. They revised the title in later editions.

Asimov often rebelled against editorial guidelines, writing what he wanted to and then hoping that editors would come around. Svirsky envisioned the book as the story of science in the twentieth century, while Asimov took a longer, historical view. He organized the book from the universal to the personal, starting with the universe at large and ending with the human brain.

The author also panicked a bit when Svirsky suggested cutting the book in half and adding an introduction by geneticist George Wells Beadle. They compromised by splitting Asimov's large work into two volumes, and Asimov eventually agreed to the introduction. Even as he worked on the final proofs, or galleys, Asimov disliked Svirsky's cuts but eventually gave in. Still, he was never fully satisfied with the first editions of the books. Both were published in 1960 under the subtitles *Physical Sciences* and *Biological Sciences*.

Overall, the books were a success and received praise from critics and scientists. Asimov was proud

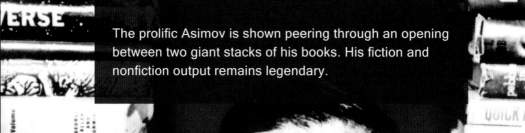

The prolific Asimov is shown peering through an opening between two giant stacks of his books. His fiction and nonfiction output remains legendary.

of a review from George Gaylord Simpson, an eminent and influential paleontologist, who called him a "natural wonder and a national resource." *Science* magazine called it "something new in popular science writing...For at least one reviewer who started with a considerable allergy toward all popularized science, the world will never be quite the same." Asimov's love for learning the subjects involved, and his skill at being "a great explainer," shone brightly from this point on. Throughout the 1960s, he would apply this talent to many topics.

SCIENCE FACT VS. SCIENCE FICTION

During this new chapter of his life, Asimov not only found great joy in writing but also found it easier. Science fiction put many demands on him, he realized later, that nonfiction did not.

First, nonfiction demanded much less brainstorming and thinking on his part. Gone was the need to plot out stories, character motivations, or neat endings. Every fiction story had to be different from the last one. Plus, once it was completed, it could not be revisited. Another drawback was the very idea of changing his fiction after completion. He hated arguing endlessly with Campbell or other editors about revisions, additions, or deletions to a particular story.

Nonfiction was quicker, with all the information already in his head or easily researched. Facts and scientific principles did not change, unlike plots. Asimov could also work on many nonfiction projects at once. With fiction, he could only juggle one story and novel simultaneously. Otherwise, he would confuse plots and characters. In *I, Asimov*, he observed, "If I were writing on vitamins in one essay and on stellar evolution in the other, there was no chance of confusing the two. I discovered I could work on many nonfiction pieces at once, switching from one to the other as it suited my convenience."

Another benefit was that nonfiction provided fresh territory for the author's imagination. He could explore new fields of knowledge. Because Asimov was always curious about almost every topic imaginable, the possibilities were endless when it came to book ideas and subjects. He also enjoyed how it expanded his horizons. The more he wrote about things unfamiliar to him, the more inspired he was to reach beyond his comfort zone. He observed that he may never have taken such intellectual journeys if he were still working at the university.

Over time, he gained a solid understanding of many fields and became an expert in quite a few. In *It's Been a Good Life*, he described how he "read biology, medicine, and geology. I collected commentaries on the Bible and on Shakespeare. I read history books. Everything led to something else. I became a generalist by encouraging myself to be generally interested in all matters."

"THE GOOD DOCTOR"

One place where Asimov shined was in the pages of *Fantasy & Science Fiction* (*F&SF*) magazine. In 1958, Robert P. Mills, who had published Asimov in *Venture Science Fiction*, asked him to do a regular column. It was a dream gig. He was allowed to write about anything he liked, for up to four thousand words per issue. From his first column on meteoric dust, Asimov wrote on subjects as varied as math, science, the environment, feminism, war, and more. Because of his friendly, conversational writing style, Bob Mills nicknamed Asimov "The Good Doctor." The 399 columns he wrote from 1958 to 1992 also kept him in the sci-fi spotlight. Doubleday regularly collected these into book editions, released almost annually for more than two decades.

ASIMOV TACKLES SCIENCE FOR TEENS

Back in 1953, Asimov had been thinking about doing books for younger audiences. That year, publisher Henry Schuman suggested he write for teenagers. Asimov was intrigued and agreed to think it over. Schuman and Asimov later dined with Schuman's science adviser, Dr. Washton. Washton told the author that when writing for teens, he should not write sentences longer than twenty-five words. Although Asimov tried it out for the first project, he later found the rule limiting. His later books for the publishers Abelard-Schuman went more smoothly when he abandoned this restriction.

The first book, 1954's *The Chemicals of Life*, was his first nonfiction for a general readership. With nontechnical introductions to biochemistry easily understood by novice science students, it was appropriate for youngsters and even adult readers eager to learn but perhaps intimidated by very technical prose. Readers learned about the human body's intake and use of chemicals in sustaining life. Asimov later credited this first book with opening his eyes to the possibilities of nonfiction, especially writing it for those without a strong foundation in the sciences.

According to the author in *I, Asimov*, the Abelard-Schuman texts were written "at the level of the bright junior high school youngster." His later works for Abelard-Schuman included books on genetics (*Races and People*, in 1955), nuclear physics (*Inside the Atom*, in 1956), and organic chemistry (*The World of Nitrogen*, in 1958), among others. He wrote eight in total in the 1950s.

Asimov did not believe in talking down to teen-age readers, another reason why he refused to dumb down his sentences; although he did avoid long, run-on sentences. "I do not simplify my vocabulary" for teen readers, he wrote. He did not think of young readers as children. At most, he included the pronunciation of technical terms to give young readers a proper introduction to unfamiliar words and concepts and thus ease their anxiety about them. Asimov's philosophy was that although teens lacked experience, they did not lack intelligence or reasoning ability.

THE BIBLE AND SHAKESPEARE

Asimov was perhaps not a natural candidate to provide a comprehensive study of the Bible. He was a humanist and nonreligious since childhood. However, his natural curiosity and prior knowledge made the project interesting to him, as did his Jewish roots. Split into two volumes—the Old Testament in 1967 and the New Testament in 1969—*Asimov's Guide to the Bible* was later released in a combined edition that numbered almost 1,300 pages. He paid special attention to history, geography, politics, and other factors behind the stories in the Bible.

Not long after, Asimov took on one of the most ambitious projects of his career, a study of William Shakespeare, history's best-known English-language playwright. It took him two years to complete. Published in 1970 in two volumes, it took a different approach than previous works on Shakespeare, dividing thirty-eight plays into four sections, according to the geographic location or era of the plays' settings: Greek, Roman, and Italian in Volume 1 and the "English" plays in the second.

True to his usual focus on making the book's topic clear to newcomers, Asimov included maps and figures to help explain the places, times, mythology, legend, and history behind each play. He did not analyze the plays but provided rich background and anecdotes. At 750 pages, it was a giant work. Still, each play received about twenty to forty pages of coverage and was listed in historical order, more or less, for each subcategory. Asimov said it was the work that gave him the most joy because he had liked Shakespeare since he was a boy. Both his Bible and Shakespeare guides still appear on college curricula worldwide.

ASIMOV EXPLAINS THE SCIENCES

Asimov's science books often covered both current and historical explorations of theory and discovery. In *Photosynthesis* (1969), he discussed the chemical processes by which plants help sustain all of life on Earth, including providing food and oxygen. A later book, *How Did We Find Out About Photosynthesis?* (1989), looked at the history of the discoveries that led to the current theories and understanding of the topic.

The work was one of several books that used the "How Did We Find Out About…" framework. He traced these phenomena from the earliest ideas of ancient civilizations to the present day and covered topics such as electricity, energy, nuclear power, and solar power. In 1984, he explained computers and a subject even closer to his heart in *How Did We Find Out About Robots?* He once said he envisioned the nonfiction science book as being as dramatic as his fiction, "with science as the hero, and ignorance as the villain."

ANY SUBJECT UNDER THE SUN

Asimov covered an astonishing range of subjects throughout the 1960s and beyond. A reader interested in any field of knowledge can pick one, and it is likely that Asimov has covered it in a book, an article, or an essay: numbers theory, biochemistry, physics, the solar system, ancient Greece and the Roman Empire, the environment, nuclear weapons, genetic effects of radiation, evolution, dinosaurs, European and U.S. history, minerals, energy, black holes, and many more.

CHAPTER SIX

GRAND FINALES FOR THE GRAND MASTER

T he 1970s saw more milestones for Isaac Asimov. Through love and loss, through illness and recovery, he kept writing as much as possible. As he entered the twilight of his years a living legend, he even returned to his roots with even more critical and commercial fame to follow.

A RETURN TO SCI-FI

In 1972, Asimov published the critically acclaimed novel *The Gods Themselves*. Inspired by a discussion on a nonexistent element, plutonium-186, the book tells the story of a plot by beings from a parallel reality who attempt to save their universe from destruction but only at the cost of risking the destruction of the sun and thus Earth itself. Asimov considered it his favorite science fiction novel, and

Oliver Platt *(center)* is flanked by actors Robin Williams *(left)* and Kiersten Warren in full robot costume in the film *Bicentennial Man* (1999), based on Asimov's story.

critics agreed: it won both the Hugo and Nebula Awards for best novel in 1973.

Another Asimov sci-fi favorite appeared in the title novella from the 1976 collection, *The Bicentennial Man and Other Stories*. In the story, Andrew is a robot trying to become human, despite prejudice and mistrust of robots. Some critics considered it a commentary on racial discrimination, and it remains a fan favorite. The story was expanded in a 1992 novel that Asimov cowrote with Robert Silverberg, *The Positronic Man*, and later adapted into a 1999 feature film.

A SEPARATION, AND REMARRIAGE

By the late 1960s, Isaac and Gertrude Asimov's marriage had begun to fall apart. There were many reasons for their eventual separation. Asimov himself blamed his own workaholic nature, which left little time for family. Others have pointed out that they grew apart and wanted separate things. They had reportedly stayed together for the sake of their children, as many couples did, but by the summer of 1969, the writing was on the wall.

With Asimov already mourning the recent death of his father, Judah, the Asimovs separated and filed for divorce. During this time, Asimov left Boston for New York. The negotiations to divide their assets that followed were difficult, and they argued often in person, on the phone, and through their lawyers. Their haggling dragged on for a few years.

Janet Jeppson welcomed her old friend to New York during his separation and soon put up Asimov at her apartment. Jeppson was a doctor and writer, and she had met Asimov at a sci-fi

convention in New York in 1956. They became close friends on the circuit over the next thirteen years. At some point after the Asimovs' separation, they became romantically involved. On November 16, 1973, a divorce settlement was finally reached. On

After his earlier marriage fell apart, Asimov found the love of his life with Janet Jeppson, a writer and doctor.

November 30, Asimov married Jeppson in her New York apartment.

BACK TO HIS ROOTS: FOUNDATION AND ROBOTS

Asimov did not slow down much with age. A heart attack in 1977 did not prevent him from putting out about ten books annually in the coming years. According his 1992 *New York Times* obituary, he once told an interviewer in 1984, "Writing is more fun than ever. The longer I write, the easier it gets." He said this not long after a triple-bypass operation in late 1983.

For decades, publishers, fans, and friends had tried

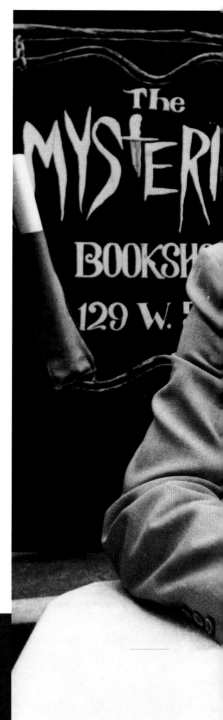

Asimov signs copies of *The Roving Mind* in 1984, during the Fifth Avenue Book Fair in New York City. In this collection of essays, Asimov criticized the growing conservatism in politics during the early 1980s.

to get Asimov to take up the Foundation series once again. In 1981, even with a large advance from his publishers at Doubleday and the promise of great success, it still took Asimov months to truly start a new novel. The thrifty Asimov felt great pressure to turn out something good, especially with so much money paid up front. *Foundation's Edge* was published in October 1982. To Asimov's surprise, the book debuted on the *New York Times'* best-seller list and stayed there for twenty-five weeks, the first of his books to do so. It was declared a powerful return to form for one of the masters of the genre. It was followed by *Foundation and Earth* (1986), *Prelude to Foundation* (1988), and the posthumously released *Forward the Foundation* (1993).

THE LIGHTER SIDE OF ASIMOV

Asimov was well known for his humor as a teacher, public speaker, and convention-goer. He did not restrict himself to educational nonfiction or thought-provoking sci-fi. Some of his favorite books to work on included ones on jokes and limericks. *Isaac Asimov's Treasury of Humor*, published in 1971, and *Isaac Asimov Laughs Again*, released in 1992, included jokes of all kinds, puns, limericks, and funny stories.

Pictured here are cast members of a British production of *The Mikado*, one of many Gilbert and Sullivan comic operas that Asimov enjoyed.

True to form, Asimov was more thorough than most writers, who would be satisfied with simply listing the material. Instead, he not only explained what made the jokes funny but also instructed readers on how they should be told.

Another love of Asimov's was the nineteenth-century theatrical team of Gilbert and Sullivan and their comic operas. He joined the Gilbert and Sullivan Society in the 1970s, and he was a regular attendee at their meetings and performances. He also knew many of their songs by heart.

SCI-FI CONVENTIONS

For much of his career, Asimov enjoyed science fiction conventions and related events, such as awards ceremonies. He was very outgoing and enjoyed the company of fellow authors, fans, and others involved in the genre. Often, he was the toastmaster, the person who would introduce speakers and make announcements at events, including the World Science Fiction Convention.

Fans found him to be approachable, and he was more than happy to autograph photos and books whenever he attended. Asimov was a main attraction at conventions, whether or not he had released work in the genre. Attending was a way of staying up on the current trends in science fiction. It was also a convenient way to see fellow author friends whom he may not have seen otherwise, including Robert Heinlein, Arthur C. Clarke, Frederik Pohl, and Sprague de Camp, as well as friends such as publishers Lester del Rey and Judy-Lynn del Rey. He corresponded with readers and fans frequently, and he responded to fan mail and answered questions through handwritten postcards.

Asimov understood the importance of conventions for the fans themselves. Attendees gained the same sense of community and belonging that the Futurians and other science fiction clubs of his youth offered.

MENSA AND THE HUMANISTS

Asimov was vice president of Mensa International, the most famous high-IQ, or genius, society. He enjoyed his membership but resented feeling like a "marked man at meetings," he wrote. Other members, especially new or younger ones, tried to challenge him or prove themselves, creating a negative atmosphere. Asimov felt that a high IQ was hardly a sign that any two people would get along.

He was also president of the American Humanist Association. He agreed with the group's stance that humanity should behave ethically and try to improve the world without necessarily having to believe in a particular religion. Humanists believe that human creativity and thought are the most important aims that people should strive for. Asimov gave many talks and produced a few books on humanism.

In *It's Been a Good Life*, he stressed their value for young fans and teens especially.

Conventions are excellent for networking, good for aspiring writers and other artists to meet like-minded people and make lasting friendships, or for simply talking about stories and books. For young people, meeting their heroes is both exciting and inspiring.

ILLNESS AND DEATH

Asimov's health declined in the 1980s. Earlier heart trouble made it necessary for him to undergo heart bypass surgery in 1983. He also had suffered from kidney stones all his life, but these had often passed very quickly. In his late sixties, several bouts of kidney disease left him hospitalized. Asimov had always enjoyed rich food and had only truly started following a sensible diet late in life, at Janet Asimov's encouragement.

During this time, Asimov barely left the house. He experienced prostate trouble around 1991 and he had begun to need a cane while walking. An assistant began taking dictation to type up his stories because his hands shook so badly.

He made one of many hospital visits in the spring of 1992 because of a sudden nosebleed, not expecting that it would be the last time. On April 6, 1992, the world learned that Isaac Asimov had passed away at the age of seventy-two. Ten years later, his widow revealed that Asimov had in fact died from complications arising from acquired immunodeficiency syndrome (AIDS), which he had contracted through an earlier blood transfusion during bypass surgery.

ASIMOV'S IMPACT

Asimov's works in science fiction and science fact have had a powerful impact on fiction writing, nonfiction, and science education well into the twenty-first century. Critics point out that many smart and ambitious science fiction franchises of the last few decades owe much, or at least some, of their structure and concepts to Asimov's Robot novels, the Foundation series, and his other works. These include the original 1960s *Star Trek* television series, along with its later versions, and the even more successful *Star Wars* franchise.

His Robot stories and novels were extremely influential. The Three Laws of Robotics influenced much of the sci-fi media that followed, including characters from *Star Trek* and *Star Wars*, the androids in the *Alien* series of films, and the works of dozens of other sci-fi authors throughout the twentieth century, including Philip K. Dick, whose own robot story influenced the groundbreaking film *Blade Runner*. The films *Bicentennial Man* (1999) and *I, Robot* (2004), starring Will Smith, are two of the few true adaptations of Asimov's works onscreen.

Even the award-winning economist Paul Krugman declared recently to the *Guardian* newspaper that he decided to enter his field largely because of Asimov. In the novels, the statistician and scientist

Actor Will Smith attends a press conference to promote *I, Robot*, the 2004 film loosely based on Asimov's robot stories.

Hari Seldon develops psychohistory, combining history, statistics, and sociology to accurately predict how very large populations in the Galactic Empire will behave in the distant future. The possibility of this kind of power inspired Krugman's imagination that his chosen field of economics could affect the real world in positive ways. Krugman may have agreed with Asimov when the author told the BBC, "Everything I write is intended to enlighten, even my science fiction. That doesn't mean, you understand, that it does enlighten, but that's its intention."

Although his science fiction stirred the imagination of millions, his nonfiction books were perhaps even more influential. While Asimov lived, technological and scientific advances occurred seemingly faster than they had during any previous period of human history. The average person, untrained in science, may occasionally have been overwhelmed by these dramatic changes.

Asimov's books were also important introductory texts for budding scientists. From teenagers to college students, his books were excellent companion works to more technical and specialized texts. His

Asimov, who made no great assertions about his own writing, relaxes on a divan. According to his obituary in the *New York Times*, Asimov said in 1984, "I try only to write clearly and I have the very good fortune to think clearly so that the writing comes out as I think, in satisfactory shape."

love of, and curiosity about, the subjects involved was contagious. He described his process as one of reading "a dozen dull books and making one interesting book out of them."

His own need to know was a driving force, too, and he put himself in the place of the new reader. He was always happy to read more on any topic to clarify it for himself, too. Mostly, he was obsessed with imparting this new knowledge to others. In April 1992, he was quoted by the *New York Times* as saying, "I'm on fire to explain, and happiest when it's something reasonably intricate which I can make clear step by step. It's the easiest way I can clarify things in my own mind."

TIMELINE

1920 Isaac Asimov is born—as Isaak Yudovich Ozimov—on January 2 in Petrovichi, Soviet Union.

1922 Isaac's sister, Maya, is born.

1923 The Asimovs immigrate to the United States, settling in East New York, Brooklyn.

1931 Isaac writes "The Greenville Chums at College," one of his first real stories.

1932 Isaac enters high school at the age of twelve.

1935 Isaac receives his first typewriter as a gift from his father.

1937 Isaac begins "Cosmic Corkscrew," the first story he will submit for publication.

1939 Asimov publishes his three first stories in *Amazing Stories* and *Astounding Science Fiction*. He enters the graduate program in chemistry at Columbia University.

1941 Asimov publishes "Nightfall," one of his most acclaimed stories.

1942 Asimov begins dating Gertrude Blugerman; they are married on July 26, 1942. He begins the Foundation stories. He leaves Columbia University and starts working at the Philadelphia Naval Shipyard as a chemist.

1945 Asimov is drafted into the U.S. Army, just after the end of World War II.

1946 Asimov is released from military service and returns to Columbia University.

1947 Asimov obtains his Ph.D. in chemistry.

1949 Asimov becomes a biochemistry instructor at the Boston University School of Medicine (BUSM).

1950 Asimov publishes his first novel, *Pebble in the Sky*, and a collection of his Robot stories, *I, Robot*.

1951 The Asimovs' first child, David, is born on August 20; *Foundation* is published.

1952 Asimov collaborates with fellow BUSM instructors on *Biochemistry and Human Metabolism*; *Foundation and Empire* is published.

1953 *Second Foundation* is published.

1954 Asimov publishes *The Chemicals of Life*.

1955 The Asimovs have their second child, Robyn, born on February 19. Asimov receives tenure at BUSM, becoming an associate professor; he sells his first science essay, "Hemoglobin and the Universe."

1956 Asimov first meets Janet O. Jeppson.

1958 Asimov leaves BUSM and begins writing full-time.

1959 Asimov writes *The Intelligent Man's Guide to Science*.

1963 Asimov wins his first Hugo Award, for his collected essays in *Fantasy & Science Fiction*.

1966 The Foundation series is awarded the Hugo Award for Best All-Time Series.

1969 Asimov's father, Judah, passes away. Gertrude and Isaac Asimov separate, beginning divorce proceedings.

1972 Asimov returns to the science fiction novel with *The Gods Themselves*.

1973 Asimov and Gertrude settle their divorce; he marries Janet Jeppson on November 30.

1983 *Foundation's Edge* is published and becomes a best seller.

1986 *Foundation and Earth* is published.

1992 Asimov passes away on April 6, 1992, at the age of seventy-two.

GLOSSARY

AGCT Short for Army General Classification Test, the AGCT measures the I.Q. and related abilities and talents of army personnel.

biochemistry The study of how chemicals work within living organisms, including humans.

dissertation A long academic essay or work on a particular subject, often a requirement for someone seeking a Ph.D., or doctoral degree.

draft An earlier, unfinished version of a published work.

fan Short for "fanatic." A person with an intense interest in something, such as science fiction or another genre, art form, or even particular writers, musicians, or other artists.

hard science fiction A genre of science fiction that emphasizes scientific or technical detail and accuracy.

Hugo Award An annual set of awards given for achievement in science fiction and fantasy.

humanism A system of thought that centers on humans, their creativity, and abilities, without considering religion or other spiritual beliefs.

jovial Positive, cheerful, and friendly or full of good humor.

limerick A type of humorous poem consisting of five lines.

Mensa International The world's largest and oldest society comprised of individuals with extremely high IQs.

periodic table The table listing the known chemical elements of the universe, organized according to their properties, and used extensively in the sciences, especially chemistry and physics.

popular science Scientific literature or material interpreted for and aimed at the general public.

prolific Refers to a large or productive output of creative works.

psychohistory A fictional mix of history, sociology, and statistics that plays a major role in Asimov's Foundation series of novels.

pulp Short for pulp magazine, pulp refers to the inexpensive fiction magazine that popularized science fiction, fantasy, and adventure throughout the first half of the twentieth century.

quarantine The separation of sick individuals from healthy ones in order to prevent the spread of contagious diseases.

robotics A term coined by Asimov in his Robot stories, referring to the branch of technology dealing with the creation and behavior of robots.

tenure The privileges given to university instructors who reach a certain level, including job security and higher pay.

FOR MORE INFORMATION

American Mensa, Ltd.
1229 Corporate Drive West
Arlington, TX 76006-6103
(817) 607-0060
Website: http://www.us.mensa.org
Mensa International is a group made up of high-IQ, or
genius, individuals that promotes studies of intelligence and group dialogue.

Canadian Science Writers' Association
P.O. Box 75, Station A
Toronto, ON M5W 1A2
Canada
(800) 796-8595
Website: http://sciencewriters.ca
The Canadian Science Writers' Association pro-
motes excellence in science communication
in Canada.

Science Fiction and Fantasy Writers of America
(SFWA)
P.O. Box 3238
Enfield, CT 06083-3238
Website: http://www.sfwa.org
The Science Fiction and Fantasy Writers of America

supports, promotes, and advocates for its members and holds the annual Nebula Awards.

SF Canada
7433 East River Road
Washago, ON LOK 2B0
Canada
Website: http://www.sfcanada.org
SF Canada is a professional association for writers of speculative fiction. It promotes the genre and advocates for its membership throughout Canada and worldwide.

Washington Science Fiction Association (WSFA)
11801 Rockville Pike #1508
Rockville, MD 20852
Website: http://wsfa.org/site
The Washington Science Fiction Association is the oldest science fiction club in the Washington, D.C., area.

World Science Fiction Society
P.O. Box 426159
Kendall Square Station
Cambridge, MA 02142.
Website: http://wsfs.org

The World Science Fiction Society is a literary society that runs the annual World Science Fiction Convention, or Worldcon, which awards the annual Hugo Awards.

WEBSITES

Due to the changing nature of Internet links, Rosen Publishing has developed an online list of websites related to the subject of this book. This site is updated regularly. Please use this link to access the list:

http://www.rosenlinks.com/GSW/Asim

FOR FURTHER READING

Analog and *Isaac Asimov's Science Fiction Magazine. Writing Science Fiction and Fantasy.* New York, NY: St. Martin's Press, 1993.

Asimov, Isaac. *Asimov Laughs Again.* New York, NY: HarperCollins, 1992.

Asimov, Isaac. *Asimov's Chronology of the World: The History of the World from the Big Bang to Modern Times.* New York, NY: HarperCollins, 1991.

Asimov, Isaac. *Asimov's Guide to the Bible: Two Volumes in One, the Old and New Testament.* San Antonio, TX: Wings Press, 1988.

Asimov, Isaac. *The Currents of Space.* New York, NY: Tor Books, 2010.

Asimov, Isaac. *The Foundation Novels.* New York, NY: Spectra, 2008.

Asimov, Isaac. *I, Robot.* New York, NY: Spectra, 2008.

Asimov, Isaac. *In Memory Yet Green.* New York: Doubleday, 1979.

Asimov, Isaac. *Isaac Asimov's Guide to Earth and Space.* Robbinsdale, MN: Fawcett Publications, 1992.

Asimov, Isaac. *The Robots of Dawn.* New York, NY: Spectra, 1994.

Asimov, Isaac. *Understanding Physics (Motion, Sound, and Heat/Light, Magnetism, and Electricity/The Electron, Proton, and Neutron).* New York, NY: Dorset Press/Barnes & Noble, 1988.

Card, Orson Scott, Philip Athans, and Jay Lake. *Writing Fantasy & Science Fiction: How to Create Out-of-This-World Novels and Short Stories*. Cincinnati, OH: Writer's Digest Books, 2013.

Datnow, Claire L. *American Science Fiction and Fantasy Writers* (Collective Biographies). Berkeley Heights, NJ: Enslow Publishers, 1999.

Hoppa, Jocelyn. *Isaac Asimov: Science Fiction Trailblazer* (Authors Teens Love). Berkeley Heights, NJ: Enslow Publishers, 2009.

Hoppenstand, Gary. *Pulp Fiction of the 1920s and 1930s* (Critical Insights). Amenia, NY: Salem Press, 2013.

Kaku, Michio, and Jess Cohen. *The Best American Science Writing 2012*. New York, NY: Ecco Press, 2012.

Patrouch, Joseph, Jr. *The Science Fiction of Isaac Asimov*. New York, NY: Doubleday, 1974.

BIBLIOGRAPHY

Asimov, Isaac. *Asimov's Galaxy: Reflections on Science Fiction*. New York, NY: Doubleday, 1988.

Asimov, Isaac. *I, Asimov*. New York, NY: Bantam Books, 1995.

Asimov, Janet Jeppson. *It's Been a Good Life*. Amherst, NY: Prometheus Books, 2002.

Detjen, Jim. "Isaac Asimov: The Complex Made Clear." *Philadelphia Inquirer*, April 7, 1992. Retrieved September 15, 2013 (http://articles.philly.com/ 1992-04-07/news/26003545_1_isaac-asimov -teaching-biochemistry-prestigious-hugo-award).

Guardian. "Great Voices of Science Fiction." May 14, 2011. Retrieved September 20, 2013 (http:// www.theguardian.com/books/2011/may/14/ science-fiction-authors-interviews).

Krugman, Paul. "Paul Krugman: Asimov's Foundation Novels Grounded My Economics." *Guardian*, December 4, 2012. Retrieved September 10, 2013 (http://www.theguardian.com/books/2012/ dec/04/paul-krugman-asimov-economics).

Leshi, Nick. "The Simple Brilliance of Isaac Asimov." Salon.com, July 27, 2009. Retrieved September 17, 2013 (http:// open.salon.com/blog/kikstad/2009/07/27/ the_simple_brilliance_of_isaac_asimov).

McDowell, Edwin. "Asimov Is Celebrating 300th
Book's Publication." *New York Times*, December
17, 1984. Retrieved October 1, 2013 (http://
www.nytimes.com/books/97/03/23/lifetimes/asi-v
-300th.html).

Miniscule, Caroline. "Isaac Asimov: A Life of the
Grandmaster of Science Fiction." Thunderchild.com,
2006. Retrieved September 9, 2013 (http://
thethunderchild.com/Reviews/Books/NonFiction/
Biographies/IsaacAsimov.html).

Pfeiffer, John. "Robots Are to Be Applauded, Not
Feared." *New York Times*, November 13, 1960.
Retrieved September 20, 2013 (http://www.nytimes
.com/books/97/03/23/lifetimes/asi-r-guide.html).

Popova, Maria. "Religion vs. Humanism: Isaac Asimov
on Science and Spirituality." Brain Pickings, August
13, 2013. Retrieved September 21, 2013 (http://
www.brainpickings.org/index.php/2013/08/13/
isaac-asimov-religion-science-humanism).

Rothstein, Mervyn. "Isaac Asimov, Whose Thoughts
and Books Traveled the Universe, Is Dead at
72." *New York Times*, April 7, 1992. Retrieved
September 28, 2013 (http://www.nytimes.com/
books/97/03/23/lifetimes/asi-v-obit.html).

Stone, Pat. "Science, Technology, and Space: The
Isaac Asimov Interview." *Mother Earth News*,

September/October 1980. Retrieved September 14, 2013 (http://www.motherearthnews.com/nature-and-environment/science-technology-isaac-asimov-zmaz80sozraw.aspx).

Suellentrop, Chris. "Isaac Asimov: How *I, Robot* Gets the Science-Fiction Grandmaster Wrong." Slate.com, July 16, 2004. Retrieved September 3, 2013 (http://www.slate.com/articles/news_and_politics/assessment/2004/07/isaac_asimov.html).

Warzel, Charlie, and John Herrman. "Isaac Asimov's 1964 Predictions About 2014 Are Frighteningly Accurate." BuzzFeed, August 28, 2013. Retrieved September 28, 2013 (http://www.buzzfeed.com/charliewarzel/isaac-asimovs-1964-prediction-of-2014-is-frighteningly-accur).

White, Michael. *Isaac Asimov: A Life of the Grand Master of Science Fiction*. New York, NY: Carroll & Graf Publishers, 2005.

INDEX

ABOUT THE AUTHOR

Philip Wolny is a writer from New York. From childhood, he was an avid reader of science fiction and fantasy and discovered Asimov's Foundation novels at an early age. He remains a fan of the genre and of the Grand Master himself. Wolny has also written a book for young adults on fantasy writer James Dashner.

PHOTO CREDITS

Cover, p. 1 Frank Capri/Archive Photos/Getty Images; p. 4 Deniseus/Shutterstock.com; p. 5 Mondadori/Getty Images; pp. 10–11 Library of Congress Prints and Photographs Division; p. 12 The East New York Project; p. 16 Transcendental Graphics/Archive Photos/Getty Images; p. 19 Jim.henderson/Wikimedia/File:Boys HS Putnam Av jeh.jpg/CC0 1.0; p. 25 © Mary Evans Picture Library/The Image Works; p. 28 George Marks/Retrofile RF/Getty Images; p. 33 © RIA-Novosti/The Image Works; p. 39 Wikimedia/File:Heinlein-decamp-and-asimov.jpg; pp. 40, 82–83 Used by permission of Special Collections & Archives, UCR Libraries, University of California, Riverside; pp. 44–45 Keystone-France/Gamma-Keystone/Getty Images; pp. 47, 70 Courtesy Everett Collection; p. 50 Private Collection/Photo © Christie's Images/The Bridgeman Art Library; pp. 52–53 © travellinglight/Alamy; p. 60 Barry Winiker/Photolibrary/Getty Images; pp. 63, 80–81 Hulton Archive/Getty Images; p. 65 Sovfoto/Universal Images Group/Getty Images; pp. 66–67 Everett Collection/SuperStock; pp. 84–85 © AP Images; p. 87 GAB Archive/Redferns/Getty Images; pp. 92–93 Koichi Kamoshida/Getty Images; pp. 94–95 © Alan Carey/The Image Works; cover and interior design elements Featherlightfoot/Shutterstock.com (fractal patterns), Peter Jurik/iStock/Thinkstock (nebula), RoyStudio.eu/Shutterstock.com (canvas texture).

Designer: Michael Moy; Editor: Kathy Kuhtz Campbell; Photo Researcher: Amy Feinberg